The Transfortainer

HOW TO HAVE BIG IMPACT AS A SMALL BRAND BY BRINGING JOY AND MEANING TO YOUR AUDIENCE

MATS PERSON

Copyright 2021 @MatsPerson

All rights reserved. No part of this book may be reproduced in any form or by any electronic or mechanical means, including information storage and retrieval systems, without permission in writing from the publisher, except by reviewers, who may quote brief passages in a review.

ISBN 978-1-304-72262-1

Imprint: Lulu.com

Edited by Sarah Busby and Andrew Dawson

Front cover design by Mats Person

Book interior design and illustrations by Mats Person

www.matsperson.com

> "ALL OF MY WORDS, IF NOT WELL PUT NOR WELL TAKEN, ARE WELL MEANT."[1]
>
> Woody Guthrie

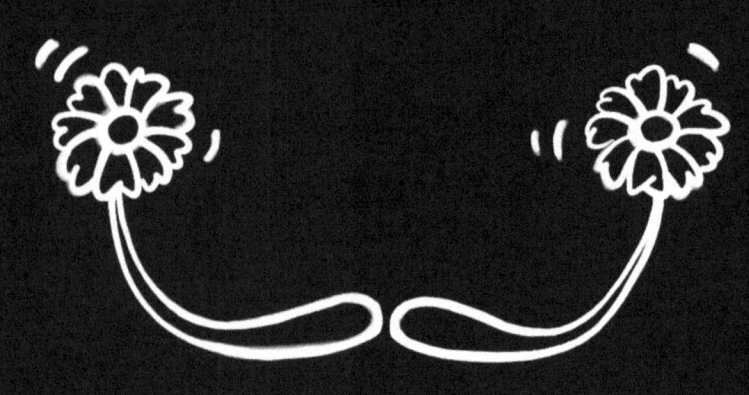

When I think about all the heroes I've had in my life, I find they all have one thing in common.

They're all entertainers in one way or another.

They've been my teachers, parents, partners, colleagues and friends. Others have been artists, filmmakers, ad men and ad women, gurus, musicians, entrepreneurs, writers, philosophers, photographers, comedians and many other things. Some I've been lucky to know or briefly meet in real life. Others I've known through their work. They are a completely diverse bunch of people, from antiquity to the modern day and from all corners of the world. And they've all arrived in my life with a totally different story to tell. But, more than this, they've made me grow as a person in some way – to become a better me. And they've done this while making me laugh, cry, dream, love, desire, plan, take action and change my ways. By consciously or unconsciously doing two things simultaneously, entertaining and transforming me, they've had a lifelong impact on me and even made me feel capable of heroic acts from time to time.

So, this book is written in their honour.

Here's to the transfortainers. Thank you, and long may you live to inspire others.

Mats Person, 2020

Content

INTRODUCTION

Who is this book for and what does it aim to do? — Page 07
Who do I think I am? — Page 09

SECTION 1: ENTERTAIN CHANGE

What's up with brands today? — Page 13
The risks of purpose-driven marketing — Page 15
Turning their 'why' into your opportunity — Page 17
Beyond purpose-driven brands — Page 19
Understanding the purpose-seeking audience — Page 21
Selling the 'who' rather than the 'what' — Page 23
What's next? If you know 'who', you'll know 'how' — Page 25

SECTION 2: TRANSFORTAINMENT

The 'who' and the 'how' build the brand — Page 29
What's transfortainment? — Page 32
Why entertainment? — Page 33
The combination punch of 'who' and 'how' — Page 35
The influencer as entertainer — Page 36
Comparing the purpose-driven and the transfortainer brand — Page 37
The transfortainer in relation to brand archetypes — Page 39
How can transfortainment be used with your brand archetype? — Page 40

SECTION 3: TRANSFORTAINMENT IN ACTION

Who's getting it right? — Page 44
Oatly - Transfortaining the dairy sector — Page 45
IKEA - Transfortaining the retail sector — Page 47
BrewDog - Transfortaining the alcohol sector — Page 49

Mailchimp - Transfortaining the B2B sector　　　　　Page 51

SECTION 4: LET'S PUT ON A SHOW

Let's put on a show　　　　　Page 55
How to become a transfortainer brand:
a brainstorming tool　　　　　Page 57

T is for Teacher　　　　　Page 59
R is for Relatable　　　　　Page 61
A is for Authentic　　　　　Page 63
N is for Non-political　　　　　Page 65
S is for Supporter　　　　　Page 67
F is for Facilitator　　　　　Page 69
O is for Original　　　　　Page 71
R is for Relentlessly consistent　　　　　Page 73
T is for Tough　　　　　Page 75
A is for Artist　　　　　Page 77
I is for Innovator　　　　　Page 79
N is for Non-conformist　　　　　Page 81
E is for Energetic　　　　　Page 83
R is for Relaxed　　　　　Page 85

SECTION 5: SUMMARY

The 'who' summary　　　　　Page 89
The 'how' summary　　　　　Page 91
The end and a new beginning　　　　　Page 93

Credits . Recommended reading and listening　　　　　Page 95
Endnotes　　　　　Page 97

Intro

"ENTERTAINMENT AND LEARNING ARE NOT OPPOSITES; ENTERTAINMENT MAY BE THE MOST EFFECTIVE MODE OF LEARNING."[2]

Herbert Marcuse

Who is this book for and what does it aim to do?

This book is for the small, entrepreneurial brand builder, start-up or upcoming but ambitious challenger brand. It's for the underdog that needs a boost to compete better with, and possibly overtake, some of the big legacy brands, despite their budgetary might.

Right now, I believe that there's a real opportunity in brand building and brand storytelling, because so many of the big brands have, in my opinion, taken their eye off the ball. And that's something you can take advantage of.

Now, the fact that I'm even suggesting this means that all the big brands who read this will switch off and put the book down right here. After all, they pay their brand consultancies millions to tell them that what they are doing right now is correct. Surely they must be right and I must be wrong? But I'm not so sure. I believe that many brands just aren't seeing what's happening to the branding space or they aren't willing to consider alternatives. This means that you and I can have this book all to ourselves; we can keep all the possible advantages for our own benefit. This gives you, the plucky new brand, a chance to get ahead of the slow behemoths. However, the purpose of this book isn't to try to prove that something is right or wrong. Instead, it's meant to act as an instigator to thinking differently and taking advantage of a possible opportunity.

As an entrepreneur or bootstrapper, you're also more likely to be equipped with a mind that's always looking for ways of doing things a little differently. If that's the case, you just might find this book useful. To keep it short and sweet, this book is simply about one thing: your future brand approach and how to refocus it for a more competitive edge.

Everything you're about to read and discover is based on a very straightforward idea driven by both personal experience and a new wind of brand thinking that's blown in and is just starting to pick up.

I've come to notice that some of the most effective brands of the new era seem to combine two existing marketing ideas. One is very new and based on the latest understanding of audience behaviour; and one goes back to the dawn of civilization – the human need to imagine and share in the imagination of others. Or, to put it in a more contemporary context, to feel joy through entertainment. It's in this intersection of the two where I think real opportunity lies for the future of brands.

Will this book deal with reputation management strategies and high-level business strategies? Thankfully, no. Nor will it deal with the details of tactics, formats and fonts. Instead, it deals with the simple human truth of brands. Simple, yet seemingly very hard to get right for some brands who focus so hard on their own outcomes that they fail to consider the outcomes for their audiences. While most books on brand building focus on your organisation's values, this one chooses to focus on the other, often forgotten (and more creatively difficult) part where the audience meets the brand. At the end of it you should hopefully be able to out-think your competition, if not yet out-spend them.

If you have more entrepreneurial smarts, desire and passion than money, then take a leap with me and consider a new path to engage your audience. And to the big brands: if you don't want to be left begging for scraps at the table of attention and engagement in the future, then I'd recommend coming with us.

Who do I think I am?!

Why on earth would a Swedish art and creative director write a book about branding for small start-ups and challenger brands? Frankly, who do I think I am?

Well, for starters, having worked for 25 years as a creative in London's advertising world, I've spent thousands of hours working on hundreds of brands. I'm also a passionate observer of audience behaviour and culture. I guess I'd have to add that I generally have a different mindset to others (some might say obstinate) that struggles with the idea of following the brand herd. Instead, I'm always on the lookout for how we can break the rules and put things together in a new and better way.

I'm also a bit of a brand 'fan', which means that anyone who starts out on the journey to build a new and genuine brand automatically has my respect. By reading this book, you are setting out on this voyage of discovery, and I want to help you as much as I can.

Now, let's push the marketing boat out from the shore and enjoy ourselves on the sea of creative possibility.

Section One

ENTERTAIN CHANGE

STOP SELLING THE WHY.
START ENABLING THE WHO.

What's up with brands today?

To understand what's happening with many big brands today, we can take a sneak peek at how they structure their brand playbooks – the document that lays out how their brand should be presented publicly – and subsequently their world view.

They are telling because they tend to have one thing in common: they almost always start with the brand itself. They will cover things like brand DNA, purpose, legacy, value foundations, role and unique selling propositions (USPs) at length. Audience considerations usually come later, just ahead of fonts and colour palettes. This approach is sometimes referred to as 'inside out'. It places the audience *after* the brand. And creative is, often, an add-on.

'So what?' you might ask: these are just brand books, and we shouldn't read too much into how they're structured. Well, to me it's an insight into how brands today tend to organise themselves around purpose-driven models, with a reliance on the same approach towards marketing as a result. By focusing on their own core values and their reason for being, they sometimes forget who the story is for.

In his brilliant book, *Start with Why*, Simon Sinek sets out how many great brand leaders work from their purpose outwards in order to express the meaning of their brand beyond just making money. The aim is to engage people in the emotional resonance of their goals. And this is important because the emotional part of the brain is also the decision-making part. This approach has therefore been the strategy *du jour* for some time now. Few brands haven't joined in with the 'emotional marketing anchored by a passionate purpose or cause' chorus.

There is a commonly-held belief that this is what audiences need to be deeply engaged with brands. But, if you look closer, while at first appearing to be focused on the needs of the audience, this model is in fact forcing the brand's gaze inwards.

In the brand's own eyes, this might not cause a conflict as long as their purpose or cause is one which the audience also feels passionate about. In fact, there's a belief that it will act as a beacon that'll draw in audiences and make the brand credible and, as such, trusted or even admired.

But something has changed since Simon Sinek wrote the book. A vast number of brands have now jumped on the purpose-driven marketing bandwagon. Inevitably, they have the same or very similar purposes and as such, tell very similar brand stories. As too many brands have started to pull on the same heartstrings, their audiences are starting to suffer purpose-driven marketing fatigue.

Thomas Kolster outlines this current phenomenon in his visionary book, *The Hero Trap*, where he says: *"Today purpose has become mainstream, and organisations trying to outcry each other in their societal efforts seem only to garner more cynicism from people."*[3]

So, perhaps purpose-driven marketing has run its course? Or perhaps purpose is still highly relevant, but brands have been looking for it in all the wrong places? Perhaps it's time to turn to the back pages of the brand playbook for once and have a closer look at that audience again.

After all, if a tree that falls in the forest when no one is there doesn't make a sound, then so too will your brand fall silent unless it connects with the audience in a way that really matters *to them*.

The risks of purpose-driven marketing

So, then, perhaps the first risk to purpose-driven marketing is the difficulty of standing out and being believed when everyone is shouting the same thing. If your brand's USP is connected to a purpose or cause shared by many other brands, then by definition it is not unique and as such no longer a USP at all.

We've also discovered that there's likely to be a general fatigue among audiences who are being approached with the same type of purpose-driven brand communications again and again. No wonder, then, that they're immune to its effects or, at worst, actively dislike and distrust these brands. This is already a massive risk for the big brands, who've all spent the last few years rewriting their manifestos to fit current trends. And for you, as a small start-up, these risks are even greater because you need to stand out even more to obtain true and valuable engagement. But there might be another risk, that is perhaps even greater, of carrying on down this path. This brings us to the topic of this book. It's the risk of ignoring those back pages in the brand playbook. Because, as you probably know, we live in an age where audiences are increasingly dominating and indeed, even co-authoring brand experiences in the form of social conversations and user-generated content (UGC), for example. To keep creating a new brand using the 'inside out' model in an increasingly 'outside in' world would seem very risky indeed.

And last but not least, there's the risk of whether purpose-driven marketing really works. Do people really buy and act on purpose as much as the current marketing mantra says they do? A *Harvard Business Review* article from August 2019 on the gap between intention and action puts some doubt in the mix. Their survey found that there is a big difference between what brands people *say* they intend to buy from (65% said they wanted to buy from purpose-driven brands) and what brands they *actually* buy from (only 26% actually bought from purpose-driven brands). [4]

So, what does this all mean?

Those brands that risk betting everything on their purpose unicorns may increasingly struggle to be heard in the future.

This is where the opportunity lies.

Turning their 'Why' into your opportunity

With purpose-driven marketing still touted by many as the most effective strategy to follow, it's easy to see how smaller new brands can be swept up in the *zeitgeist* and feel they have to do the same. Many are still writing or rewriting their manifestos along these lines.

I've worked with many big brands who have gone through this process of readjusting their brand stories to fit current narratives. I've seen examples of what can go wrong along the way. Typically, they begin by finding an issue or cause that is considered important to the audience. They then use that issue as a way to re-establish a 'why' for their own brand. It's easy to see why big brands do this. They think that 'taking the lead' on the issues their audience cares about will add to their credibility, and this, in turn, will encourage the audience to follow them. The hope then is for the brand to be positioned as a purpose or cause leader. If the new-found purpose shows virtue, it also seems like a quick win in terms of appearing current and progressive. But the question we need to answer is: how credible is it to an audience (who hates dishonesty and adores authenticity) to retrofit a purpose? If the brand truly believed in their retrofitted purpose, why wasn't it founded on that purpose? And why did the marketing department have to come up with it? It may seem smart but ultimately, it's manipulative and self-serving, and your audience likely knows that.

This leads us to the bit where you can have a real opportunity. When many of the big legacy brands abruptly change their supposed purpose, they don't just provoke massive questions around authenticity, but they may also create a clash of purpose. The greatest example of this surely must be Gillette's 2019 US advert about 'Toxic masculinity' created to re-launch Gillette's male shaving products under the new slogan 'The best men can be'. The TVC was hugely criticised for gender stereotyping and it created a big backlash for Gillette. YouTube comments were negative 10 to 1. Their sales and market share also fell although there are various and contradicting figures on this. But it's probably safe to say it's been very expensive for Gillette both in terms of sales and reputation. The brand's desired outcome, or new 'why', was to be seen as a leader in shaping cultural masculinity. The problem was, this was massively at odds with the audience's own desired purpose and outcome.

The purpose of this book however is quite clear. And it is not to criticise Gillette or any other specific brands or indeed their views or actions. But instead to shine a light on what's really interesting about this for you the small brand. And it is that all of these risks, or blunders when clumsily put into practice, equals a massive potential opportunity for you.

My first thought when the Gillette ad broke wasn't whether its content was right or wrong. It was, what competitors are going to take full advantage? With thousands of angry men swearing they'd never use Gillette again, the opportunity was there for the taking. Dollar Shave Club was first out of the gate with its simple tweet 'Welcome to the Club' - holding its welcoming arms out to any disgruntled male looking for a new shave brand. As a smaller competitor this is obviously the kind of opportunity you dream of. And here's the best bit. As long as the big legacy brands try to lead with 'why' focused and purpose-driven marketing, they will also most likely continue to make dubious marketing calls from time to time and open up space for their competitors. It doesn't matter what sector your brand is in. There are examples in most of them, of big brands who got it wrong. All you need to do is to be ready when they do. But it's important to note that I'm not talking taking an opposing political stance (See page 65) - No, all you need to do is what Dollar Shave Club did.

Provide a safe haven away from brands who will continue to try to claim leadership. And instead be the brand who provides support for an audience that is seeking its own purpose.

Beyond purpose-driven brands

As we've seen, what we face right now is a brand landscape where an ever-increasing number of brands are telling very similar stories with louder and louder voices, and with fewer and fewer people actually believing what they say.

So, what can you do to take advantage of this moment in time? What can you pursue instead of a purpose-driven brand narrative? Well, firstly, I'm certainly not saying that your brand shouldn't have a purpose. As long as it's authentic (meaning you'd act in a purposeful way even if no one was listening), then I'm all for it. Purpose *does* matter. But there is an important question to ask. Namely, how much longer will virtue or purpose on its own remain a *differentiator*? Most brands can't just rely on their purpose to be their entire brand identity in the long term.

To truly understand the shift we're facing, we must get our heads around the fact that brand virtue will very soon be taken for granted. It will be the norm. It will not get you noticed and talked about. It won't win you gold stars with your audience. Instead, they will *expect* your brand to be ethical, high quality, fair and for it to do right by the world. At most, in the future, purpose will be just a tick box for an audience checking a brand's credentials. But beware, credentials are never the brand story.

So, what *does* the new audience want instead of purpose? The answer is simple. They want the story to be about *them*. Your brand's role is now to enable them to become the person they want to be. Or, as Simon Sinek argues in his speech about Millennials, '*This Is Why You Don't Succeed*', new audiences crave the ability to make an impact themselves. [5]

If you care about your audience, you need to understand the shift that's happening. It's less and less about *your* purpose and *your* status as leader, and it's ever more about theirs.

Welcome to the purpose-seeking audience.

"WE'RE THE MOST ETHICAL AND GREEN BRAND!"
"WE'RE THE FAIREST AND GREENEST OF ALL!"
"NO WE'RE THE FAIREST GREEN BRAND EVER!"
"LOOK AT US, WE'RE SO MUCH MORE ETHICAL!"

Understanding the purpose-seeking audience

"MILLENNIALS DON'T JUST WANT TO READ THE NEWS ANYMORE. THEY WANT TO KNOW WHAT THEY CAN DO ABOUT IT."[6]

Ian Somerhalder

As digitally native audiences have already entered their 30s, we need to understand that they have grown up with a certain amount of power at their quick-swiping fingertips. They are ultra-aware of themselves, and they hate being told what to do and believe. And they really don't like being pigeonholed, preached to or bored. They are the 'slashie' audience, and thus they believe they can be whatever they want to be. If that happens to be a dentist 'slash' super car vlogger or marine biologist 'slash' model, then it's their choice. More importantly, they want to save the world while doing it. This is why what they seek is *their* purpose and not *yours*.

From their point of view, it's all about what they want to become rather than what your brand wants them to become. You have to fit them and not the other way around. The only way for your brand to matter is if it enables them to become the star in their own movie.

And if your brand still insists on prioritising social change and its own purpose, remember the wise words of author Deepak Chopra: *"Unless there's a personal transformation, there can be no social transformation."*[7] So there's no way around it. If you don't impact your audience by giving them personal value, you're not going to impact society either.

It looks like the old adage 'the customer is king' has finally come true at long last.

Selling the 'who' rather than the 'what'

In his book, *The Hero Trap*, -Thomas Kolster tells us: *"Instead of asking why you exist as an organisation, always ask who you can truly exist for."*[8] As we leave purpose-driven marketing behind, this perfectly encapsulated the shift in focus to attracting purpose-seeking audiences. Brands should no longer sell 'things' or their own purpose; instead, they should enable a transformative experience or provide personal value for their audience. Wise brands now sell the 'who' you want to become.

Let's consider this in practice. For example, instead of being in the business of building greener cars, your brand should now, most likely, be in the business of enabling greener drivers. Or instead of being a 'farm fresh vegetables' delivery service, you should probably now be in the business of creating accomplished vegan chefs. The starting point is the audience's desired transformation. Only once you have established their 'who' should the brand provide a supportive and enabling nudge towards its promise. To get this balance right requires deep insight. But those brands that dig deep and get to know their audience well enough will find there's a real reward in finding that their 'what' has become a 'who'.

But this new 'who' goes deeper in purpose-seeking marketing. It's more than just a transient feeling; it's a transformation. It's about real change as opposed to a fleeting moment. It's about a closer connection to the brand, with the product or service feeling increasingly incidental. For an audience that craves 'personal purpose' and 'impact', this is what will draw them in.

What's next? If you know 'who', you'll know 'how'

What brands need to do now is to place the brand focus where it has to be: their audiences' needs. It's time to temporarily put aside your business' needs so as to make sure you have a business in the future. But, once we know how to offer the audience what it wants, how do we best communicate that?

As professor of network science, Albert-Laszlo Barabasi, writes in his book, *The Formula*: *"Your success is not about you, it's about us."*[9] What his research on the science of success shows is that any type of success is based less on our 'performance' and much more on *how it is received* by an audience.

In other words, it's in the act of receiving that an audience determines what a brand will mean to them. It's the vibe as much as the message itself, the *how* as much as the who, what or why.

The time has come, then, for all brands to start becoming interesting and exciting. And not just to themselves but to their audiences. In doing so, they become someone audiences would like to hear from and hang out with. It's important to consider that our image is decided by what the audience thinks of us, not what we think of ourselves. Several great brand thinkers, from David Ogilvy to Marty Neumeier, emphasize that brands are in fact the consumer's idea of a product or service, much more than the brands' own ideas of themselves. To be thought of as truly interesting might therefore seem difficult to achieve, but there's a way to do it successfully. And it takes you into a space where only a few brands so far have ventured. In a landscape full of often preachy or sentimental marketing, they shine brighter.

In the next part of the book, we'll hear from the brands that tell stories of how *and* who; the stories that entertain *and* change.

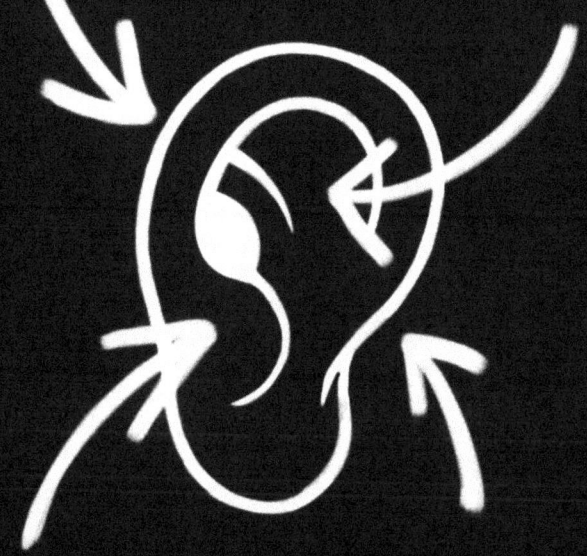

Section Two

TRANSFORTAINMENT

> **"WE NEED TO STOP INTERRUPTING WHAT PEOPLE ARE INTERESTED IN AND INSTEAD BE WHAT PEOPLE ARE INTERESTED IN."**[10]

Craig Davis - Former CCO of JWT

The 'who' and the 'how' build the brand

So, how can we be sure that this 'who and how' thinking is right? Do we really just have to focus on entertaining our audiences with stories that place them firmly at the centre of our brand universe? It would certainly seem too simplistic to some who are used to more complex models of brand creation. Well, I believe that, as always, it's the audience we need to ask. According to statista.com, the most popular online activities for US adults in November 2019 were:

1) Communicating with friends/family via messaging (92.3%) or email (90.3%)
2) Watching online videos (74.3%)[11]

And if we then look at *why* people love watching online videos almost as much as chatting to their friends, we find that the number one reason is to be, you guessed it, entertained.
In January 2020, 53% said seeking entertainment or inspiration was their main motivation for engaging in online videos, according to supercoolcreative.com.[12] Learning something new was the main motivator for 21% of respondents.

As we are at the time of writing, gripped by a global pandemic, current statistics might be a little unusual. We know, for example, that e-commerce has blown up the internet over the last year. As have online entertainment services. But there is very little evidence to make us doubt that the underlying emotional motivations of people will change. Audiences will certainly keep seeking out that which entertains them and enables them to become the person they want to be.

These two truths are the pillars of the concept of 'entertaining change' – the importance of brands offering both authentic transformation and entertainment in order to speak to what our audience most desires. Or, as I like to call it: transfortainment!

"A good teacher, like a good entertainer, must first hold his audience's attention.

Then he can teach his lesson."[13]

John Henrik Clarke

ENTERTAIN (V.)

late 15c., "to keep up, maintain, to keep (someone) in a certain frame of mind," from Old French entretenir "hold together, stick together, support" (12c.), from entre- "among" (from Latin inter; see inter-) + tenir "to hold" (from Latin tenere, from PIE root *ten- "to stretch").

What is transfortainment?

Transfortainment is entertainment with the distinct purpose of giving transformative value to an audience. Okay, so transfortainment is perhaps a bit of a monstrosity as a word. But I think we need to give this approach a name. It deserves it.

Arguably, it combines two of the most effective ways we know to encourage an audience to give brands their true attention, engagement and ultimately, trust and loyalty.

The first part – empowering the audience by enabling personal transformation – requires that brands reposition themselves from audience leaders to audience enablers. This means creating a framework where the audience can be the hero and drive their own personal destiny.

The second part – entertainment – is the way in which it's done. Namely, through effective storytelling which will captivate and move the audience. This aims to put them in the right frame of mind to absorb the message and enable change.

I should say that, when I talk about entertainment, I don't mean the Saturday night TV format of sparkly suits, dad dancing and bad jokes. Incidentally, some confused brands still think this makes for good advertising and brand communications. I mean entertainment in its true and original form. In other words, the ability to put someone in a very specific and *positive* frame of mind, and then keep them there.

Brands are no longer makers of things. The great ones are broadcasters, entertainers and purveyors of emotional value.

Why entertainment?

We have already discussed the importance of the first pillar of audience transformation: the 'who'. Now let's turn our attention to the second one: the 'how'. Why is entertainment so important and effective as a tool to reach and engage audiences?

Some would argue that this approach seems old fashioned. Now you know what your audience wants, surely there's a more scientific way to capture them than stories? They would say things like: 'We use data to precisely target our audience with highly contextually relevant content.' But when we say things like this, we are still thinking with a 'catch' mindset, meaning it's still about the brand trying to catch you, the audience, when it thinks you're most receptive to receiving its message and choosing its offerings. This, to some of us, is still push marketing – hard selling and overbearing. If you've read this far, I assume your thinking is more like mine, that of a *creative brand builder*. Because what we're after is contextually relevant **and** entertaining content that draws in the audience. In the attention economy we find ourselves in, constantly *chasing* people for attention is backing a lame horse. Or, as Jeff Bezos says (and what entrepreneur would argue with him?): *"Advertising is the price you have to pay for having an unremarkable product or service"*[14]. And if I may Jeff, I'd like to add "unremarkable brand".

And it's true to say that every remarkable brand that's ever existed has known about the importance of being able to entertain. The fact that entertainment is as old as Moses *is* exactly the point.

It's the most enduring way to get attention ever conceived. Why? Because it's utterly human at its core. And it's all about *pull*.

"WITHIN ALL AREAS OF THE INTERNET, ENJOYMENT IS MANDATORY" [15]

Alexander Bard and Jan Soderqvist - Digital Libido

Let's consider some of the reasons why creative entertainment is so effective at pulling us in:

- We seek it out without prompting (Netflix and YouTube viewing was up 15-30% in 2020 alone).

- It cuts through the noise of daily life and pulls us in (689 million monthly TikTok users globally in 2020 came only to be entertained).

- An entertaining story or message ranks as the most likely way to earn consumers' attention (according to Celtra, 2020).[16]

Brands that authentically entertain are those that people seek out, love to spend time with and can't wait to get back to. So if you want to stop having to pay for every second of engagement and every hard-fought click, you need to consider how to start expressing your brand creatively.

The brands that get this right know that entertaining content:

- Engages audiences more deeply.
- Causes audiences to dwell longer and return without being prompted.
- Puts audiences in a relaxed frame of mind and allows for transformative content to be organically absorbed.
- Simply put, makes audiences *like* brands.

The combination punch of 'who' and 'how'

Woody Guthrie was a singer songwriter during the great depression who believed in social justice for the poor and unemployed. He understood that, in order to reach an audience with his political message, he had to be entertaining or it simply wouldn't register with them. In fact, he saw his role as both educator *and* entertainer. Responsible for contributing to social change during his life, his legacy is still felt to this day with his 'people's' anthem, *This Land Is Your Land*. It was deliberately created as an easy sing-a-long tune so it would live forever more around campfires and in classrooms. So, there's nothing new here. We've just forgotten how to do it.

As Herbert Marcuse said: *"Entertainment and learning are not opposites; entertainment may be the most effective mode of learning."*[17] And as learning is key to personal empowerment, it's pretty clear there's no better way to give transformative value to an audience than combining it with an entertaining approach.

Let's explore this idea of combining two ideas to create a fresh approach, a little further. In creative and innovation circles, this type of juxtaposition is commonly used to make someone think and feel they are exposed to something completely new. For example, I've used this idea to tell the story of this book (combining a new need for personal transformation with a timeless behaviour, entertainment). And I'm not alone. Think of Spotify. They combined an audience's love of listening to music with their social desire to share music. Two old behaviours became one new one, and it changed the way people behave around music.

If you're a start-up, chances are you've already been through a similar innovation process. You've looked at existing behaviours and what new solutions can be introduced to satisfy those in a new and exciting way. So, let's use that same 'combination' thinking to create your brand story.

The influencer as entertainer

If you still doubt this whole argument, let's take a look at one of the biggest marketing phenomena of the last 10 years. Namely, the influencer. Think about it for a moment. Influencers inspire, teach, empower and transform their adoring audiences. And they do it by being entertaining. Influencer marketing takes full advantage of this. Influencers' unique value proposition is clearly important, but to underestimate the underlying value of entertainment is a huge mistake. For example, when Adobe (software for creatives) teamed up with Casey Niestat (who has 12.3 million YouTube subscribers as of April 2021) it was a match made in heaven. Known as a creative type, Casey draws an audience that comes to be entertained (the 'how') but that ultimately wants to be a creative like him (the 'who'). And since Adobe has the exact same goal , it's easy to see the potential of the partnership.

We can see that entertaining is an effective method of telling the story of the brand. So why do so few brands seemingly want to take this approach? I suspect that, in the era of purpose-driven marketing, many brands have become so focused on *what* their story is that they've forgotten *how* to tell it. In fact, over the last 10 years in advertising I've noticed a real decline, not just in the desire to entertain, but also in the ability to be creative. Meaning the ability to create stories that resonate, engage and entertain.

Instead, it's the influencers' content that now pulls in audiences, by the millions every second. Brands rely on sponsoring them, effectively outsourcing this role of creative entertainer. Surely, it's high time for brands themselves to re-learn this art?

Purpose-driven brands are still the norm, but transfortainers are already everywhere around you and gaining ground quickly. Now let's imagine a high-level fictional example to demonstrate how these techniques might play out in the real world.

The purpose-driven vs the transfortainer brand

Let's compare these two approaches by imagining that we've created an ultra-sustainable menswear brand for adults 35-44.

THE WAY OF THE PUROSE-DRIVEN BRAND

THE BRAND:
- Very focused on its USP of ultra-sustainability.
- Has superb credentials in the form of a transparent supply chain and super low emission.
- Sees itself as a leader in new markets that lots of people talk about.
- Knows its audience is interested in building a sustainable wardrobe.

Results in: WHAT focus
- Very keen to share its sustainability creds with an audience, its thinking is 'Inside out'.

THE BRAND COMMS:
- The brand creates communications around sustainable menswear, supply chains, their low emissions and carbon footprint.
- Having painted itself into a corner with a one-dimensional story, it now has nowhere else to go other than more talk of reducing its carbon footprint which is difficult to make entertaining.
- These stories risk being skipped by the audience.
- It uses paid-for 'push' tactics in desperation.
- It pushes ever harder with its credentials content.

THE AUDIENCE:
- Our target audience persona, David, wants to update his wardrobe.
- He cares about his carbon footprint, and budget.
- He shops for sustainable menswear brands but skips our brand because he's bored with 'depressing' conversations around environmental collapse and dull scientific content.
- He is drawn in by entertaining, personally inspiring content by a cheaper brand.

Results in:
- He buys from them instead.
- David feels a little bad that he ignored the sustainable brand, but he's glad he saved money.

THE WAY OF THE TRANSFORTAINER BRAND

THE AUDIENCE:
- Our audience persona John, wants to overhaul his wardrobe to fit his new job, believing this will give him more confidence in his role.
- He cares about his carbon footprint.
- He wants to become a more stylish, suave and confident version of himself.
- John loves Steve McQueen and 007 films where cool men's styles come alive.

Results in: WHO focus
- The brand learns who the audience are and who they want to become.

THE BRAND COMMS:
- By knowing *who* he wants to become, the brand now also know *how* to talk to him.
- It creates entertaining content featuring classic suave men's style tailored to John's taste.
- It 'enables' John by providing wardrobe planning guides and creating 'looks' where each outfit has a combined carbon breakdown.
- It makes it entertaining through immersive and artistic content that John seeks out for joy.
- John buys pieces directly from social media, while he is in an inspired state of mind from interacting with this content, despite the higher cost of the brand.

THE BRAND:
- The brand used an 'outside in' approach and didn't lead with its credentials story.
- The brand not only made a sale but created a fan relationship and an ongoing support role to John.

Results in:
- The brand now has an enabler position that supports their audience's outcomes e.g. 'Enabling confidently dressed men to live sustainably'.

The transfortainer in relation to brand archetypes

Those familiar with brand building will be aware of the 12 brand modelling archetypes. Whether it's the hero, the outlaw, the jester, the creator, the ruler or the magician, these personas are often used to position a brand and define its values and behaviours. However, behaving like a transfortainer is not at odds with this type of modelling and should be seen instead as complementary or even an improvement. The biggest difference with the transfortainer approach is that it positions the brand with the audience's needs and personality as its starting point.

The transfortainer could at first glance be confused with the traditional brand model archetype, the jester, but has in fact much in common with the multifaceted personality of the true original – the medieval court jester. Shakespeare described the court jester as *"being the only one in the court wise enough to play the fool"*.
In short, in a world where the audience is king, the court jester, because of his unique position and entertaining delivery, is the only one that has the king's attention and trust. In this position of power, he is able to utilize all of the best qualities of the archetypes to harness this influence.

The perfect transfortainer therefore straddles several of the brand archetypes:

He cuts through the noise with joy like the jester.
He gets your attention like the rebel.
He breaks rules like the explorer.
He connects emotionally like the lover.
He speaks the truth like the innocent.
He inspires greatness like the hero and the creator.
He enables like the magician.
And he builds trust like the everyman.

How can transfortainment be used with your brand archetype?

The magician can become a successful transfortainer as long as the audience is made to feel part of the solution.

The lover is a natural fit since they already deal with human emotions. Just remember to give transformational value as well.

The hero can make an amazing transfortainer but *only* if the brand remembers that the audience is the new hero.

The rebel makes for a perfect transfortainer with his ability to disrupt norms. But he must avoid taking himself too seriously.

The innocent speaks the same pure truth as the transfortainer, but watch out for tendencies to become too 'saintly'.

The explorer is a good fit with the transfortainer approach. While they share non-conformity at their core, it's important to invite the audience in and let them be part of the story.

The jester, as discussed, has the 'how' nailed down in using entertainment to influence and gain trust. All he needs to do is up his 'who' game.

The creator shares his fundamentals like authenticity and creativity with the transfortainer. With transformation at his core, the creator only needs to make sure he also entertains.

The everyman can easily become a transfortainer by focusing on the transformative value they give to the audience. Often what people want to become is rooted in earthy, practical pursuits.

The sage, ruler and caregiver are, in my opinion, too far away from the transfortainer to easily incorporate his approach. But even so, do experiment with some 'who' and 'how' thinking.

Section Three

TRANSFORTAINERS IN ACTION

"WE TRY NOT TO ACT LIKE A COMPANY."[18]

Michael Lee – Creative Director, Oatly

Who's getting it right then?

In the following pages, you will find a selection of brands who, in my opinion, have managed to do an amazing job in combining transformative value with an entertaining approach. To me, these brands all act as transfortainers.

There could have been so many brands here if only they hadn't lost their way. Once glorious companies have frittered away their lead in the market because of an eagerness to position themselves as noble leaders instead of focusing on and empowering their audience. And as much as this is sad to see for a brand lover like me, it's great news for you since it opens up space for enablers to gain ground. So, let's have a good look at what the ones that get it right have in common.

- They generate *positive* conversations (and free media).
- They get massive return on investment (ROI).
- They inspire an emotional response while delivering factual content.
- Their brand tone of voice feels like it comes from a real person, a friend even; not a corporation or a preacher.
- They make you believe you're dealing with a creative and therefore innovative bunch of people.
- Their approach feels creative, current and authentic (not contrived, navel gazing, overly emotional or retrofitted).
- They don't play on negative emotions.
- They make you happy and leave you with a smile on your face and a love for their brand in your heart.

> **"GOOD MARKETING MAKES THE COMPANY LOOK SMART. GREAT MARKETING MAKES THE AUDIENCE FEEL SMART."**[19]
>
> Joe Chernov

Oatly - Transfortaining the dairy sector

"We literally can't make the stuff quick enough."[20] So comments Michael Lee, creative director at Oatly. The brand's growth is so rapid it would make most businesses green with envy. So, what are they doing that most brands are not?

For starters, they are a typical transfortainer brand. Behind the brand is a really serious message and product that embodies their core purpose to protect the environment. They've probably done more to bring down the world's CO2 levels than many other brands combined. Their green credentials are exceptional. Yet, remarkably, they've chosen not to beat their chests in the usual dull and finger-wagging way but instead have taken a humorous approach to their brand narrative.

Outwardly, they act very much like a challenger brand. They pick fights with the dairy giants. When the Swedish milk lobby threatened to take them to court, the brand used the trial for content and advertising. More recently, in 2021, they've taken on the EU with a new marketing campaign called 'Are you stupid?' It challenges the EU's Amendment 171, which poses a number of threats to dairy alternative brands. And once again, it's a serious issue handled in Oatly's trademark whimsical and light-hearted style. Meanwhile, behind the scenes, there's serious work going on. For example, they are helping farmers turn from traditional dairy farming to more environmentally friendly methods. But whatever they do and however serious their intentions, it's always promoted with their personal style of light-hearted banter.

So, they entertain us – but how do they help transform their audience I hear you ask? Well, as we know, audiences crave authenticity and honesty. Oatly's humour isn't accidental, I suspect. It has a purpose beyond being entertaining. The brand's tone of voice of earthy honesty lays a foundation of trust with their audience who sees them as 'real'. This then helps them follow an ethical lifestyle, while at the same time feeling part of a revolution in which honesty is paramount.

ANOTHER AD FOR OUR OAT DRINK PROVIDING NO REASON AT ALL WHY YOU SHOULD TRY IT.

IKEA - Transfortaining the retail sector

'Live Unboring' is IKEA's mantra. With these simple words, they're positioning themselves as true transfortainers. Everything they do has a sense of fun and possibility. Yet, underneath it all, there's another story. Namely, to help 'create a better everyday life for the many people'. This is a philosophy where, for example, parents become better and more creative mums and dads. Where families get to have a more fun home life. Employees have a better work day. Or simply where people become better designers for their homes and lives.

Even back in its early days in Sweden, IKEA had a brilliant campaign line: 'Not for the rich, but for the wise.' This tapped straight into the mindset of the average Swede at the time. As citizens of a pseudo-socialist society, the Swedes frowned upon being rich, but all wanted to think of themselves as clever.

The advertising has changed many times over the years, but their core brand story of enabling everyday people to become smarter and more creative has remained. And it's always done with enough fun to fill a whole Ivar shelf unit.

So, we know they can entertain us – but do they transform us? I'd say very much so. At every touchpoint with the brand, the audience is helped to feel like 'they can' do it themselves. They somehow make normal people feel like they suddenly have DIY skills; their products are simple enough to imagine, design and build. IKEA is a great transfortainer brand, in my book. Very often entertaining but most importantly, always an enabler and supporter of people.

In short, they encourage us to feel as if we can become that handy and inventive home creator we really want to be.

BrewDog - Transfortaining the alcohol sector

I've just realized that my first two examples of transfortainer brands are Swedish, as am I. I don't want to seem biased, so my next example comes from Scotland, namely BrewDog. Their brand profile is very much that of the irreverent challenger brand, even though they're now very established and priced at a premium level.

The brand is full of entrepreneurial stories that see them triumph against the odds, and that bravery runs through their comms. Early on they used unconventional tools like crowdfunding to get things off the ground, and this made it feel like the company belonged to the fans. They've continued to foster this feeling of belonging by bringing everyday people in as investors as part of their initiative called 'Equity for Punks'. This BrewDog army of followers embodies the idea of great beer and great times.

So, how do they entertain us? Well, it's very much through an irreverent lens. When Aldi copied BrewDog's flagship beer, BrewDog responded by creating a new can called ALD IPA. The ensuing 'banter' on social media then became the brand's bread and butter for their marketing approach. When the pandemic began, they opened 102 virtual bars which brought their fans together, yet again, through their shared love for the brand and a good time. This also cemented the feeling of being part of the BrewDog 'punk club'.

But do they transform their audience? Well, as we know, before BrewDog there had been a growing trend for craft beers. This was brilliant for a niche audience of 'connoisseurs', but to the rest of us it was, well, quite dull. What I think BrewDog has done exceptionally well is to enable normal people who love a good time to discover quality craft beer without this need for special knowledge. The brand, in emanating a 'punk' attitude, has given everyday people permission to be a little bit discerning in their beer choices without the stigma of having to be a bore.

Mailchimp - Transfortaining the B2B sector

Before you say 'this is all fine, but we're a professional B2B brand that needs to be dull to be taken seriously', consider this business to business example.

Mailchimp is a brand that seems determined to think and feel like a start-up even though they've been around since 2001. The brand is currently expanding their business to offer a complete marketing platform for smaller brands but doing it using an unusually creative approach for this sector.

"Their wry sense of humor is an authentic part of their brand,"[21] says Ben Crick, a creative director at Collins who worked on the branding and their illustration style. The idea for the Mailchimp brand is to project a tone of friendliness and approachability. They do not want to fall into the trap that so many others have, that they feel they must become slick and glossy as they grow in order to convey a more corporate image.

MailChimp's transfortaining approach is perhaps best illustrated by their 'Did you mean Mailchimp?' advertising campaign by Droga5. They took a fun, sideways look at the infamous mispronunciation of Mailchimp in the credits of hit podcast *Serial* by creating a series of surreal short films. These were based on fictional companies with similar names, like Jailblimp depicting prisoners on an airship. Aside from this, they produce creative and inspiring content for their audience. So, yes, it is possible for a business to business brand to be a transfortainer.

But how do they help to transform their B2B audience? To me, it seems this takes place in two ways. Firstly, in the value they give their customers through their new style of advertising platform, which helps to transform their old customers into fully-fledged 360 marketers. The other way is through their creative and quirky approach, which is there to always inspire and entertain their audience of marketers and entrepreneurs.

Section Four

LET'S PUT ON A SHOW

"WE CREATE HAPPINESS."[22]

Walt Disney

Let's put on a show

We're finally here. You've hopefully realised that reimagining yourself as a transfortainer could indeed be the way to brand success. If so, congratulations. Welcome to the business of entertaining change.

As Gary Vaynerchuk, the in-your-face but hugely successful social media entrepreneur and brand guru, says; *"It's time to start thinking about yourself as a media company."*[23] And he's right of course. Successful brands are broadcasters. It really doesn't matter if you're starting an apple stall at your local farmer's market or if you're setting up a small tech company. Either way, if you don't understand that your first job is to broadcast your transformative value in an entertaining way, you'll always play second fiddle to those that do. So, it's time to start thinking like entertainers.

But how do we do this? In the following pages I'll outline the journey you'll need to embark on to discover the transformative value and personal meaning that your brand can give to your audience. And the entertaining way in which to do it effectively.

Now, let's put on an unforgettable show.

The audience is the hero

First, we need to cast our players in the performance. And I'm sorry, but in the show we're about to put on, you haven't been cast in the lead role. Instead, the role of hero has already been given to your audience. And the hero's story is really what will drive the narrative from here on in. Remember their need to find their own yellow brick road? Classic storytelling tells us that the hero has to have a quest and an obstacle to overcome. So does your audience. He or she has something they want to achieve, become or transform into. This can seem a bit overdramatic for our marketing purposes at first. But look more deeply and you'll find answers that will unlock who they really are. No true hero story is superficial and mundane. Rather, it's most likely about a life-defining personal change of direction. In other words, try to look at your audience with the eyes of a Hollywood scriptwriter. Then let your brand be the key to their adventure.

If you're struggling to find enough drama around which to build your brand, then look no further than the fact that people today are craving meaning in their lives. A typical First World problem is that, because we already have every material thing we could ever need or want, we are sucked into a void of feeling purposeless and directionless. The stories we tell must help to fill that void. As humans, we have to have meaning in our lives. Purpose-driven marketing has already *tried* to fill this void with pre-packaged, pre-digested and hashtag-friendly campaigns. These tend to feature the brand as the active leader, which in turn makes it easy for people to feel meaning by association when they in turn like, share, fill in petitions etc. However, this approach has, to a large degree, missed the vital point of giving the audience itself *real* meaning. The kind of personal meaning that doesn't come pre-packaged and requires more engagement than sharing a few hashtags. Association with meaning could only ever be a temporary solution for an audience that wants to be the hero.

So, what's your brand's role then? It's that most classic of roles: the trusted sidekick. Whether it's Chewbacca to Han Solo, Donkey to Shrek or Watson to Sherlock; all great sidekicks know that their role is to be that consistent, trusted and honest companion on the hero's journey. Not only will the sidekick enable the hero on the journey of transformation, but he or she will also make the journey a whole lot more fun.

Now we know what roles we're going to play, it's time for you to get in character to write or rewrite your brand's story. Next I'll set out the steps that will help to define your role and actions.

How to become a transfortainer brand: a brainstorming tool

Here is one way to inspire your thinking around your new position as a transfortainer. We'll be using TRANSFORTAINER as an acronym to pin down all the qualities and behaviours that this entails. Pick a few of these and combine them – you might even surprise yourself.

The first half of the acronym, 'TRANSFOR', relates to the first pillar of this concept: the 'who'. This covers the roles you might want to play and the things you might do to enable your audience to achieve the transformation they desire.

The second half of the acronym, 'TAINER', covers the second pillar of the concept: the 'how'. This outlines all the roles you should play to entertain your audience.

If you can embed some or all of these behaviours as you build your brand, then you might just position yourself ahead of the curve and beat your competitors.

Often {
- *T* is for Teacher
- *R* is for Relatable
- *A* is for Authentic
- *N* is for Non-political
- *S* is for Supporter
- *F* is for Facilitator
- *O* is for Original
- *R* is for Relentlessly consistent

More {
- *T* is for Tough
- *A* is for Artist
- *I* is for Innovator
- *N* is for Non-conformist
- *E* is for Energetic
- *R* is for Relaxed

T is for Teacher

BE A TEACHER. INSPIRE AND TRANSFER KNOWLEDGE.

When we turn our focus away from ourselves as a brand and start to focus on what our audience need themselves, we quickly start to discover what we need to give them. Often, this is transferring knowledge or inspiring and helping someone to learn something new i.e. teaching.

How to do it:
Your brand no doubt sits on a wealth of knowledge that your audience is thirsty for. Format this in a way that makes it accessible, inspiring, creative and enjoyable for the audience to discover themselves. But it's good to also help them to share that knowledge with others in turn. In other words, build your brand around a helpful and giving approach.

Think of serial entrepreneur Gary Vaynerchuk's mantra to give, give, give, then ask.

Example:
IKEA's lockdown campaign used their usual 'how to' instruction booklet style and created ideas that made it easy for parents to turn their IKEA furniture into forts and castles for their kids to play in while stuck at home. They focused on supporting their core audience with exactly the kind of inspiration and knowledge they needed during a difficult time.

How do they enable change in their audience?
IKEA always work to enable their audience to become better people at home. In this case, IKEA showed parents how to transform into better and more creative parents when they were facing the problem of how to keep their children occupied during a pandemic. All in an entertaining way.

FÖRTRESS

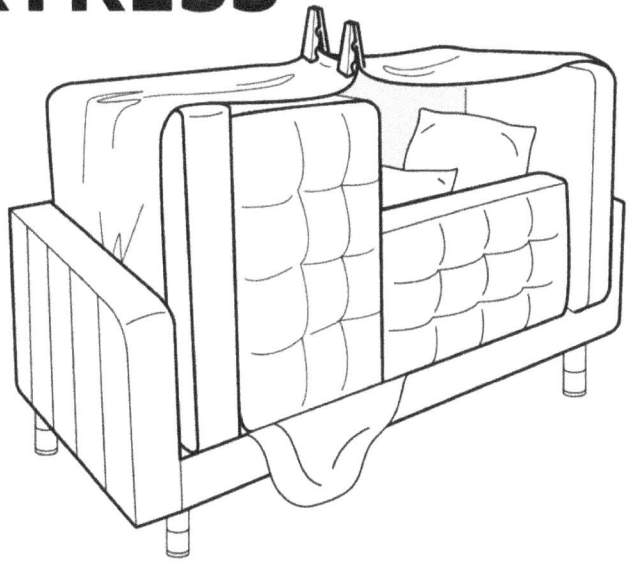

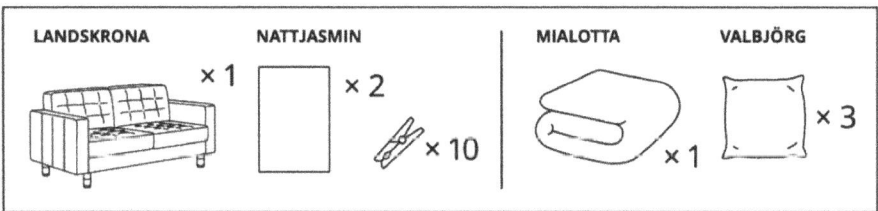

Make sure that the structure is safe. Do not leave children unattended.
The suggested examples are not ofcial IKEA user guides for IKEA products.
If you can't And the products referred to in the instructions, use similar ones.

R is for Relatable

BE RELATABLE. BE ONE OF THEM.

When YouTuber Ryan Higa (21.4 million subscribers as of December 2020) was asked to reveal the secret of his success and why so many fans are drawn to him, he simply answered: *"I'm relatable to my audience, and they are relatable to me"* [24]

How to do it:
Rapport is generally considered the most important aspect of communication. And so it is for brands as well. Once you understand how your audience wish to transform, you need to start speaking to them about it on a human level. For example, the brand story could highlight aspects of the company's own journey of transformation to build a joint space of understanding.

Example:
REI, a US-based outdoor retailer, chooses to focus its brand on kinship instead of trends. During Black Friday, they set themselves apart from everyone else in the marketplace and gave their entire staff a fully paid day off, using the hashtag #OptOutside. The idea was not only to encourage their employees to get outside, but to entice others to join in, inviting their audience to go hiking with them. Rather than just being another brand trying to encourage rampant consumerism, they felt and acted like normal people who'd had enough of the Christmas shopping cycle and wanted to reconnect with the outdoors – something their target audience could relate to.

How do they enable change in their audience?
The most loved brands are always those made up of fans themselves. Hikers want to shop with hikers, surfers buy boards from surfers, and so on. When the lines between audience and company are blurred, the fans become part of the brand's collective history, and share their values and emotional assets. Little is more powerful than when brand and fans become one.

A is for Authentic

BE REAL. BE HONEST. BE AUTHENTIC.

In any relationship, trust is at the very core. Your audience will judge your brand on everything you do. If you deserve their trust, you will eventually get it. And if you don't, you won't.

How to do it:
First of all, you must recognize that actions speak louder than words when it comes to trust. As a start-up or small brand, this is where you can really shine. We've established, it's often hard for the big brands to achieve total authenticity in the face of business realities, so they sometimes rely more on words. You can beat them and win the audience's trust by being all about action over words.

Example:
Swedish clothing brand ASKET takes this to a whole new level. With their mantra, 'The Pursuit of Less', they are literally telling their audience to buy fewer clothes. Since the real truth is that, no matter how sustainable your new fashion is, *not* buying new clothes will always be better for the planet. Through their 'care, repair, revive' thinking, they encourage responsibility for the whole lifecycle of a garment. This is an interesting stance for a company that makes its living from *selling* clothes. To remain successful, they guide their potential customers through a journey of how to create a 'buy less and keep longer' wardrobe that is full of timeless 'staples'.

How do they enable change in their audience?
When you buy an ASKET garment, it comes with an 'impact receipt' that shows you the exact cost of the garment. This is not the financial cost to the buyer, but rather the impact cost to the planet. This then enables the buyer, in a very practical way, to trace their own personal environmental impact and become that low-emissions person they crave to be.

N is for Non-political

BE TOLERANT. BE INCLUSIVE.

Tribe building has been part of many brand narratives for a long time now, and it can be effective since humans seem hardwired to feel good when they find their particular 'camp'. Over the last few years, many brands have taken this strategy to the political arena. Aside from creating a divisive world, these brand stories are likely to quickly become outdated as political winds are in constant flux. Brands can't afford to shift goalposts the way a politician or tribe can. Because every time that brand manifesto gets rewritten, there is a loss of trust and authenticity. This doesn't mean brands can't stand for something. It just means finding a way to build communities that stand for tolerance.

How to do it:
Create your own brand world where everyone is welcome. Invite 'haters' and 'lovers' both. Don't segregate, eliminate or exclude. Instead of feeding the machine of division, put all your focus on bringing people together to give a bit of joy to all.

Example:
Marmite. Their brand narrative is all about choosing what tribe you're in. Do you love it or hate it? On the surface, it might seem a divisive narrative: exactly what I was just decrying. But cleverly, they always give as much of themselves to the 'haters' as they do to their fans. Smart perhaps, because they've figured out that growth will come from those not yet convinced rather than from their existing customers. Or perhaps it works because it strengthens the love in their existing fans. Either way, it works.

How do they enable change in their audience?
In encouraging debate but keeping it fun and inclusive, they are enabling their audience to become part of a culture where we talk about our differences and enjoy opposing opinions instead of dismissing those that we don't agree with.

31ST JANUARY.

NATIONAL LOVE IT OR HATE IT DAY.

Dividing the nation since 1902.

S is for Supporter

BE ROBIN, NOT BATMAN.

As you know, your role is not that of the hero. That role is already taken by your audience. Your role is the trusted sidekick. And as such, it means you supply the canvas for them to paint on and support their journey. This is about inspiring and nudging the audience towards the transformation that they want to achieve.

How to do it:
As a true supporter of the audience's transformation, your job is to set up their experience and the emotional wins you believe they need in order to achieve their goal. Ad agency briefs used to ask 'how do you want the audience to think and feel?' They rarely do these days, and it's a shame since this is key to setting up the emotional outcome. So, start by asking how you want your audience to feel when they touch your brand? Loved, safe, hopeful, relaxed, joyful, brave, proud, energized, clever? Only when you know this will you know how to be a true supporter.

Example:
One of my favourite brands is Lurpak butter. They have done much to create braver and more creative home cooks. Their close up, energetic cooking TVCs are legendary, but so are headlines like 'PRIDE – you won't find it in a ready meal'. So, what emotional state are they putting us in when we touch the brand? Well, I feel brave, free and consequently, creative in the kitchen. And I'm sure I'm not the only one. As a true supporter, the brand sees the potential in their audience to be great home cooks before they see it themselves.

How do they enable change in their audience?
From being in fear of failure, home cooks are transformed into brave chefs who dare to tackle the trickiest of soufflés. Lurpak makes us creative, confident cooks who might burn a roast every now and then but never hesitate in giving something a good go.

F is for Facilitator

BE AN ENABLER. FACILITATE CHANGE.

This one should not be confused with the previous 'supporter' role where your job was to inspire and nudge. The facilitator role is much more concrete. This is about literally providing the tools for the transformation of your audience.

How to do it:
The word empower is thrown around a lot these days but, in my view, enable is a better word. Empowering an audience is still leaving them to sort it out themselves. Enabling someone requires a more specific offering. It is to *help* make it happen.

Example:
Toyota has a knack for using its existing customer base to help potential new customers make the right car choice. As Toyota owners are famously happy with their cars, it made sense to turn owners into an army of everyday ambassadors. For example, 'the Camry effect' was an online forum where owners shared their stories of moments with their Toyota Camry. The idea was to engage non-Camry owners through existing owners. With almost 100,000 stories shared, it was an undeniable success. Similarly, Toyota ran a brilliant campaign in Norway a few years back that brought together owners of Toyota hybrids with prospects who wanted a test drive. These unconventional approaches enabled prospects to experience the bigger story of car ownership.

How do they enable change in their audience?
For potential new customers, it helps breaks down the old preconceptions of car brands being hard to pin down and potentially a bit underhand. Instead, they are offered the possibility of a more open and honest car-buying experience. This could transform their outlook on what car buying should be and feel like, making them more confident in their choices.

O is for Original

BE DIFFERENT. BE UNIQUE. BE YOU.

To be unique requires great bravery. It means stepping out from the crowd and declaring your view of the world, without knowing whether it will sink or swim. But this is what all brands must do. You already have your own point of view driven by your unique personality. Just start using it.

How to do it:
First, get comfortable with thinking differently. This doesn't mean you have to reinvent the wheel every time. All it means is that you need to look at the same old thing from a new angle. So often the 'new' is there just waiting to be discovered. Creatives and entertainers often simply see what others don't when looking at the same picture. Start looking, playing and turning things upside down or simply repurpose something. Unique brands never follow trends. They *invent* trends for *their* audience.

Example:
Apple is a great example of this. Their unique take on personal computers and devices was driven by Steve Jobs' originality. He was famously able to combine various cutting-edge technologies and the beauty of modern design to make something truly different to what was already in the market. Like all good creative thinking, it seems so obvious now. But to do it first required that ability to see the world in a uniquely personal way.

How do they enable change in their audience?
Before being a brand for the masses, Apple used to be a product for creatives. It was technology made for people who loved a beautiful user experience. They in turn were transformed into a generation of digital creatives, that then acted as ambassadors for the brand, providing the high status and design kudos that over time has given Apple mass appeal. Now anyone can feel part of that clique and be as creative as they want to be.

R is for Relentlessly consistent

BE CONSISTENT. EVERY DAY.

Trust is what most brands want to earn from their audiences. And the biggest reason for trust breaking down is inconsistent behaviour, because your audience won't be reassured that you will give them what they need when they need it. You'll appear to be shape-shifty and unreliable. To show up consistently, with the same values and same core message, is what all brands who seek longevity must do.

How to do it:
Firstly, be consistent with your brand story. This is why your authentic purpose should never change to fit trends. Instead, make your brand story one of a simple and timeless truth that'll never go out of style, and which will never run out of angles you can tell it from. The second part is consistency in showing up. Set posting and media schedules you can stick to so that your audience knows when you will be in touch.

Example:
I'm a fan of Coca Cola's consistent brand story of joy and the feeling of happiness. Even when they move through various stages of marketing and iterations of campaigns that might highlight different aspects, such as 'Can't beat the feeling', 'Always the real thing', 'Taste the feeling' or 'Together tastes better', it's always, at its core, about human happiness and the joy of sharing. As such, they've positioned themselves deeply in our souls as enablers of feeling joy.

How do they enable change in their audience?
What human being on planet earth doesn't want to be happy? And who doesn't want to share that joy with their friends and loved ones? And what brand wouldn't love to hold this position, forever? Coke has literally created a blueprint for how humans should feel happy.

As much as we can argue that this is only cynical marketing, I'd argue it's more than that. The idea of friends and families sharing in good times and connecting through feelings of joy actually 'adds life' to their lives.

T is for Tough (and unafraid)

BE BRAVE. BE TOUGH. BE FEARLESS.

Every piece of brilliant and effective marketing or brand building ever conceived has required one or (usually) several acts of bravery. Far too often, when things go wrong, it's because of a lack of bravery. We think of comfort zones only applying to individuals, but it's very common amongst brands too. It manifests in many different ways. Fear of being first with new thinking. It's uncomfortable to risk being misunderstood. Fear of breaking away from current trends. It's uncomfortable to go against the grain. Fear of standing out and then cursing the fact that no one takes notice. There's an old advertising saying that if a new campaign doesn't make you feel nervous, it's not going to have impact. I think there's a lot of truth in that.

How to do it:
If you've ever watched great actors on stage, you'll have noticed that a big part of what makes them great is the conviction of the delivery. In fact, there's nothing worse than a nervous actor on stage. The uncertainty creeps out into the audience, where eventually it transforms into a dislike for the performer. This is also very true for brands. The ones that act with bravery and conviction always come across better to their audience. Risk-averse brands that sit back and watch their competitors step up and try new things to gauge what will work and what won't might feel safe. But in reality, it's often they themselves who end up risking the most by always working to blend in and not risk upsetting. Transfortainers, on the other hand, are always brave with their brands – just like great artists that always step up to sing that high 'C'. And, yes, sometimes we fall flat. But without risking anything, we will never be a true transfortainer either. So for you, the start-up and challenger brand, having a permanently brave mindset is a must. Stand out (fearless) emotional and practical value for your audience are key battle grounds. Areas you can and must win.

Example:
Paddy Power is a true transfortainer brand in my view. On the surface they're madcap, fun and highly entertaining. But to me, this brand is as much about bravery as it is entertainment. The brand is a manifestation of the fact that if you step up to the table and risk a little, you can achieve anything. All while having a good time. Not bad positioning for a gambling brand. Not bad at all.

How does this entertain the audience?
By coming across as a funny, entertaining and brave brand, Paddy Power inspire a fearless attitude in their audience. They enable them to go from risk averse to living that thrilling, fun-filled and free-wheeling life where taking a punt and having a go becomes part of your own persona.

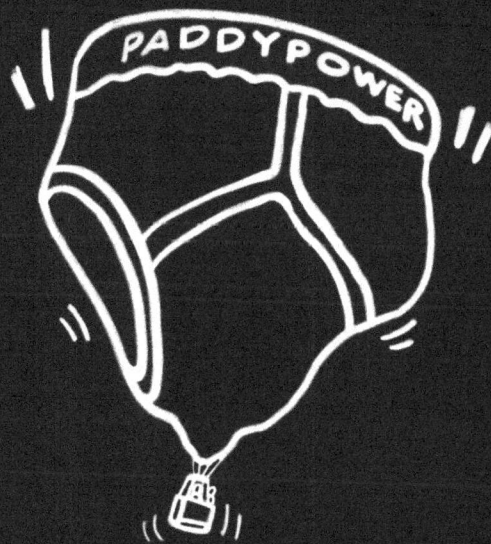

A is for Artist

BE CREATIVE. BE AN ARTIST.

Some say that brands and marketing are now all about science. No doubt science has massively contributed to our ability to understand audiences better, but sadly it's increasingly used to replace creativity. I once worked on a well-known brand where the leader of the creative group insisted on breaking down TVC scripts in Excel and analysing every individual scene against certain 'scientific' parameters. Every scene in isolation from the others. So much for the magic of storytelling and the creative artist's ability to deliver overall emotional impact by revealing the story in increments and building towards a crescendo.

How to do it:
To become an effective advertising or marketing creative is a huge undertaking, and the 'how to' would easily fill a book bigger than this one. But the good news is that the brand founder doesn't necessarily have to be a creative in their own right. What, in my opinion, is essential for the brand founder to do is to be clear about their creative ambition and set a level that always needs to be met. The reason for this, and I base this on personal experience, is that far too many brands view creativity on a sliding scale. This is bad because, once again, inconsistency is confusing for the audience. In the same way that marketers position the brand against its competitors, so must the brand position its creative level. How creative and innovative are your competitors? Do you believe that being seen as a *more* creative brand will give you a business advantage? Or will a lack of creativity not matter? The only real way to determine this is to view it in relation to what the audience wants from the brand. So, for example, if your vision is to be seen as the most innovative, your creative ambition needs to match. Because creative brands are creative in their core narrative. It's very difficult to 'add' later. You are or you aren't. Decide.

Example
In 2019, Burger King won the Cannes Lions 'creative brand of the year' award. The honour was bestowed thanks to highly creative campaigns such as 'McWhopper' (asking McDonald's to join them in creating a burger to promote World Peace Day), 'Hack Google Home' (getting Google Home devices to tell the Whopper story) and many more over the years. What it tells us is they're a brand consistently dedicated to creativity. And if you want evidence that creativity provides a business advantage, you just need to look at the numbers. The 'McWhopper' campaign earned them $220 million in free media and 'Hack Google Home' earned $135 million. Meaning that the brand generated massive news and press coverage and social media engagement organically, by getting people to talk about them.

How does it entertain the audience?
The intended target audience of early adopters aged 16-34 loved 'Hack Google Home', and made it trend across all main social platforms. The McWhopper concept captured the imagination of the world, with 8.9 million impressions, and created a 40% increase in global awareness of World Peace Day. They were drawn to this content because it entertained; a perfect example of pull marketing.

I is for Innovator

BE INNOVATIVE. BE NEW. SURPRISE.

'Newness' is proven to increase dopamine levels in humans. Hence, we love the new. Just ask a roller coaster designer. They have to rebuild their rides every so often because people can no longer get the highs they want from the same old rides. If we are able to give people something new – an alternative to the old, boring and stale – we are able to capture their imagination using this ability to stimulate and excite.

How to do it:
Common ways are to look for unexpected combinations or new applications for established behaviours and experiences. Always ask: how else can this be used? Who else can use it? How else can we do it? What collaboration or new juxtaposition can we create or invent? Almost all forms of entertainment are built on the new, from the obvious like comedy shows and live acts to things such as fashion and design. If you're one of those brands that thinks that following trends might bring you closer to your audience, I'd say that 'following' anything takes you further away from the new. Surprise yourself to surprise your audience.

Example:
I once worked on an egg brand that had a problem. They couldn't sell their extra-large eggs with the other eggs as they didn't fit in the boxes. Our solution? We repurposed these eggs as extra special baking eggs in their own extra special packs. We turned a disadvantage into an advantage by presenting these eggs as a new product. This tapped nicely into the desire for all things baking at the time of launch. Did it work? Absolutely! When all the supermarkets had sold out of our eggs, they even started producing their own brand baking eggs.

How does it entertain the audience?

'Newness' always draws in and entertains the crowds because it is inherently exciting. People will queue for hours for the thrill of a new ride, trainers or phone. They sign up months in advance for the joy of bragging rights to be the first with a new Tesla. And with our humble eggs, we managed to entertain a whole set of home bakers by positioning the eggs as must-have accessories for their kitchen and adding fashion flair to their bakes. And as with all the examples here, 'the new' just worked.

THINK ABOUT THINGS DIFFERENTLY

N is for Non-conformist

BE IRREVERENT. BE A REBEL.

Transfortainers never take themselves too seriously or slavishly follow the crowd. It's as unattractive in brands as it is in people. So, go ahead and let yourself be cheeky and irreverent in thought and action. Don't ever conform to what others think you should do.

How to do it:
For challenger brands, this is surely your bread and butter. But all brands would do well to consider this tactic. My favourite approach here is simply to ask yourself what 'the opposite' looks like? What rules can we break? It's interesting that almost every star of the current art world started out breaking all sorts of rules. The artworks of Banksy and Shepard Fairey started on dark streets, late at night, with hoodies drawn. And if you think the guerrilla marketing approach to building brands is a waste of time, then all I'll say to you is *Fearless Girl*. The bronze sculpture in Wall Street, commissioned to advertise an index fund of gender-diverse companies, generated $7.4million in free media coverage in its first month alone. Not bad for what many would describe as just a 'stunt'.

Example:
Irn Bru drinks. This totally irreverent Scottish soft drinks brand is a true non-conformist. It's a brand that's created its own little world where, just like the Scottish national psyche, freedom of expression and independence lie at its heart. Having worked on Irn Bru, I know from personal experience they are a client that encourages madcap originality more than pretty much any other brand. It was a blast for those of us who got to work with them, and it sold by the tank load.

How does it entertain the audience?
To be really loved by some, you have to be prepared to get a bit of

stick from others. So being non-conformist may put some people off, but it will win you loyalty from others who appreciate the fact you stand out. Although I'd personally stay away from being politically divisive, it can be useful to take a humorous stance and poke innocent fun, especially at other brands.

E is for Energetic

BE A SOURCE OF ENERGY. FUEL YOUR AUDIENCE.

At its very core, entertainment is a transfer of energy. Have you noticed how comedians or musicians on stage are able to invigorate the crowd? If you've ever been on stage yourself, you know the importance of kickstarting your audience with a big dollop of enthusiasm. In my view, it's the same with brands. Your brand can be a fuel for your audience to run on. And once they fill up, they start giving energy back.

How to do it:
Your brand needs to be very active and highly entertaining. So, ask yourself that question again about what emotional state you want your audience to be in. Ask yourself how you can activate your brand in a way that leaves them feeling energised. Even if your brand is slightly more sedate, you can still use energy transference as an approach. For example, you can transfer positive energy in the form of hope, or you can transform a reassuring energy in the form of increased bravery in your audience. The list can be as long as your arm. Just start giving.

Example:
This example just had to be Red Bull, didn't it? Here's the interesting thing about this brand. Not only do they sell canned energy, but the whole brand seems to radiate energy. Interacting with the brand gives you a buzz, even if you're not drinking the product. Whenever there's an action-packed event, Red Bull is there. Arranging it or sponsoring it. The brand simply owns action and energy. I had the pleasure to work as a creative on Red Bull when it made its launch in the UK. At that point, the brand had already shown a huge appetite for going where other brands wouldn't normally go. Like when we promoted Red Bull as a mixer for Vodka in clubs by drawing with lipstick on the bathroom mirrors. Something tells me it's paid off.

How does it entertain the audience?
Energy goes hand in hand with happiness, entertainment and full-on fun. But beyond the core product in the can, Red Bull are masters at putting on crowd-pleasing and entertaining events. Anything from soap box races to world-record-beating events such as their Stratos space free fall.

R is for Relaxed

BE RELAXED. BE NATURAL. BE HUMAN.

At the centre of all brand communications stand two humans talking to each other. And just as with people, we prefer brands who are relaxed and comfortable in their own skin. Far too many contrive their stories to fit certain narratives they think will make them more popular with their audiences. Instead, if you let go just a little, something amazing tends to happen. You open up the humanity of your brand. Your audience feel let in. They become co-authors of your story, and they start to feel it's their brand too.

How to do it:
In the book *Join Me,* by Danny Wallace, the main character starts a 'collective' without purpose. Remarkably, and for no apparent reason, people start to join. The joiners soon start to organise and promote 'the collective' despite not knowing its purpose. And what's interesting is that this is common human behaviour. To make sense of what seemingly doesn't make sense. To organise that which is in chaos. A classic advertising trick is to leave something out of adverts on purpose. Why, you ask? Because it invites the audience to complete the story. And as such, become part of it.

Example:
Starbucks has used this engagement approach to build natural brand authenticity. They use hashtags such as #redcupcontest (promoting their holiday drinks offering) to transform their audience into content creators for the brand. This type of user-generated content (UGC) is not unique, but Starbucks has done it better than most (#redcupcontest posts on Instagram are, at the time of writing, close to 40,000 and counting). The result for Starbucks is, of course, that their social feeds are full of content starring Starbuck's branded cups. Content that otherwise the brand itself would have to produce. But not only that; UGC gives an air of relaxed inclusivity and authenticity while at the same time delighting the audience, who have also become creators.

How does it entertain the audience?
There's nothing more engaging to an audience than to be part of the story. And you can only truly do that if you relax the brand enough to allow for co-authorship. When Starbucks created their famous #redcupcontest, they encouraged the audience not only to entertain each other, but also themselves individually by being creative with their posts. The ultimate goal for your brand is always for your story and their story to become one.

Section Five

SUMMARY

"HERE I AM, ENTERTAIN ME."

T-shirt print

The 'who' summary

THE RISKS OF PURPOSE-DRIVEN MARKETING

- A brand's purpose might not be a USP in the long term because the chosen purpose will almost certainly be shared with too many other similar brands. Ethical values, for example, will soon be the norm.

- Therefore, a brand's purpose will soon only act to make a brand credible, at best. It won't mean that you are exclusively chosen.

- The 'intention-action gap' between what brands people say they want to buy from versus those they actually buy from is close to 40%. Actions are very different from words.

- Too much focus on your brand's purpose creates an 'inside out' approach in an environment where there's an increasing demand for 'outside in' brands.

- 'Inside out' strategies can trap brands in a 'push' comms approach.

- Purpose marketing can only be an advantage if it is 100% authentic and has a natural and solid connection to the brand. If not, the audience will recognize this sort of action as inauthentic.

- A brand's purpose must be viewed as a long-term prospect. Brands that rewrite manifestos to fit current trends risk losing the trust of their audiences. What might seem like a quick win, won't be.

THE ADVANTAGES OF AUDIENCE-DRIVEN MARKETING

- Audiences are driven by their *personal need* for meaning and purpose. The brand's purpose will soon be a mere credibility tick box for the audience.

- Audiences are increasingly in charge of the conversation when it comes to brands. Brands should therefore fit the audience, and not the other way around.

- Brands that let their audience co-author are seen as more creative, authentic, human and engaging. And less as 'just a brand'.

- Audiences prefer to be pulled in as opposed to pushed toward.

- Brands that can shift their focus from themselves to the audience can gain space in the marketplace since few have shifted to this way of thinking. This is a timely opportunity.

BRAND ROLE AND POSITION BEYOND PURPOSE

- It's not about what your brand makes. It's who it makes it for.

- Smart brands will focus on being purpose enablers, not purpose leaders. This in itself can create a position for you in the market.

- An authentic purpose should be embedded in the brand, but the brand communications must involve the audience.

- Brands should never speak on behalf of their audience or position themselves as their leaders. The audience *is* the leader.

- Most purpose-driven brands will have to 'sell' based on their own 'wins'. By focusing on the audience's achievements instead, you can position yourself as an enabler brand.

- Brands that prioritize their audience will inevitably start with the moment where the audience meets the brand. Hence, they will build creativity into the core brand, story and tone. It won't be an inauthentic marketing add-on.

- Give honestly. Don't take or pretend to give, then take. If you don't care about your audience. They will know.

- Position yourself as a transfortainer. More of that next.

The 'how' summary

ALL PURPOSE AND NO FUN

- Purpose-driven marketing frequently paints itself into a 'worthy' corner creatively speaking, since its main narrative is often about 'serious' issues.

- The total range of emotional tones available for purpose-driven marketing can therefore be creatively limiting. The palette tends to be outrage, pity or sentimentality.

- Purpose-driven marketing often tries to appeal to an established consensus of opinion and as such, can struggle to feel new, fresh and creative.

- We know that what people want most from brands is creativity, authenticity and innovation – something that purpose-driven marketing does not always nurture.

THE ENTERTAINING BRAND ADVANTAGE

- Entertaining brands are generally seen as more creative.

- Time and time again it has been shown that more creative brands deliver better business results, according to Marketing Week.[25]

- By prioritizing the audience, transfortainers will consequently focus on the basic human needs of meaning and pleasure.

- TikTok is the fastest growing social media platform in the world, proving what the Ancient Romans already knew. Namely, that entertainment satisfies a basic, human need for pleasure.

- The creative transfortainer brand can paint a picture, or story, using the full rainbow of emotional colours. Joy, hope, desire, excitement, satisfaction, love, security, bravery, pride, etc.

- Entertaining brands will find it easier to create a distinct personality because of this wider scope of expression. And as such, they will stand out and get the attention that dull brands have to pay for.

- Entertainment is sought out by audiences. As such, entertaining brands benefit from deeper engagements as well as better ROI.

- Audiences seek out what they are interested in. If you become what they are interested in, they will hear you.

THE QUALITIES OF A TRANSFORTAINER BRAND

The combination of transformation and entertainment is a potent one. It delivers the 'who' and the 'how' in the way the audience wants. Below is a reminder of the actions of an effective transfortainer brand.

T is for Teacher	**T** Is for Tough
R is for Relatable	**A** Is for Artist
A for Authentic	**I** Is for Innovator
N for Non-political	**N** Is for Non-conformist
S for Supporter	**E** Is for Energetic
F for Facilitator	**R** Is for Relaxed
O for Original	
R for Relentlessly consistent	

"IF YOU DON'T DISTINGUISH YOURSELF FROM THE CROWD, YOU'LL JUST BE THE CROWD." [26]

Rebecca Mark

We've reached the end and a new beginning

You now have all the tools to be able to write your own creative brand story from the outside in. As you may have noticed, the lens has been kept wide and at no point have we discussed specific tactics and media. This has been deliberate since so many brands make the mistake of starting with the granular. So, instead of making that metaphorical child's painting where we finish perfecting the sun before we move on to the grass, we must start by sketching out the bigger picture with a large brush so as to define our overall direction. And I'm not talking about strategy. I'm talking about a high level creative vision. This is vital to understand. If you think this sounds obvious, then you should know that I've worked on big brand projects where the first point on the agenda has been to discuss what formats we should be using in the brand communications. Enough said.

I believe that if you don't start at the beginning, focusing on how to bring meaning and joy to your audience, you'll probably end up creating just another 'also' brand that has to advertise itself out of trouble. Don't let that be you.

So, best of luck to you and your new brands.

Happy creative brand building.

Recommended reading and listening

Books

Start with Why	By Simon Sinek
The Hero Trap	By Thomas Kolster
Digital Libido	By A. Bard & J. Soderqvist
Crushing it	By Gary Vaynerchuk
Storyworthy	By Matthew Dicks
Delivering Happiness	By Tony Hsieh
Loveworks	By B. Sheehan & K. Roberts
Positioning	By Al Ries & Jack Trout
Tribes	By Seth Godin
Join Me	By Danny Wallace
Velocity	By A. Ahmed & S. Olander
Hegarty On Advertising	By John Hegarty
Oversubscribed	By Daniel Priestley

Podcasts

Social minds	By Theo & Eve @ SocialMinds
The Entrepreneurs	By Monocle
Overthrow II	By PHD & eatbigfish
Social Media Marketing	By Alan Stelzner

Credits

The following photographs, illustrations and adverts were reproduced in this book with gratitude.

Unicorn photo	By Cottonbro @ Pexels
Driver photo	By Omisido @ Pixabay
Hashtag photo	By Jon Tyson @ Unsplash
Oatly photo	By Arno Senaner @ Unsplash
IKEA Illustration	By Yuelanliu @ Pixabay
BrewDog photo	By Gary Butterfield @ Unsplash
Mailchimp photo	By Norbert Levajsics @ Unsplash
IKEA advert	By McCann Tel Aviv
Man and dog photo	By Spencer Gurley @ Pexels
Marmite campaign	By Adam & Eve / DDB London
Toyota photo	By Christina Telep @ Unsplash
Apple store photo	By Zhang Kaiyu @ Unsplash
Neon sign photo	By Ivan Bertolazzi @ Pexels
London Gherkin photo	By Roman Fox @ Unsplash
Cover photo, rights incl.	By 123rf.com

All other imagery is by the Author

Endnotes

1. *Woody Guthrie quotes*. (n.d.). Quotefancy. Retrieved 02 January 2021, from https://quotefancy.com/quote/2307333/Woody-Guthrie-All-of-my-words-if-not-well-put-nor-well-taken-are-well-meant

2. *Marcuse, H.* (n.d.). Herbert Marcuse Quote. Lib Quotes. Retrieved August 15, 2020, from https://libquotes.com/herbert-marcuse/quote/lbx6b3a

3. *Kolster, T.* (Ed.). (2020). The transformative promise [E-book]. In The Hero Trap (pp. 81–82). Routledge. https://play.google.com/books

4. *White, K.* (2019, August 1). The Elusive Green Consumer. Https://Hbr.Org/2019/07/the-Elusive-Green-Consumer. https://hbr.org/2019/07/the-elusive-green-consumer

5. *Sinek, S*. (2018, December 18). This is why you don't succeed YouTube. https://www.youtube.com/watch?v=xNgQOHwsIbg

6. *Somerhalder, I.* (2013, October 2). Social good summit. Mashable.Com. https://mashable.com

7. *Chopra, D.* (n.d.). Quotes. Https://Www.Azquotes.Com/Quote/856407. Retrieved May 20, 2020, from https://www.azquotes.com/quote/856407

8. *Kolster, T.* (2020a). *The Hero Trap* [E-book]. Routledge. https://play.google.com/books

9. *Barabasi, A-L.* (2019) *The Formula* [E-book] Pan Books

10. *Davis, C.* (2016, September 27). Interruption marketing. Collectivecontent.Co.Uk. https://collectivecontent.co.uk/2016/09/27/craig-davis-on-interruption-marketing/

11. *Statista.* (2019, November 27). Internet activities of U.S. users 2019. Statista.Com. https://www.statista.com/statistics/183910/internet-activities-of-us-users/

12. *Murdico, D.* (2020, January 28). 9 Reasons People Watch Online Videos. Supercool Creative Agency. https://supercoolcreative.com/9-reasons-people-watch-online-videos/

13. *Clarke, J.* (n.d.). John Henrik Clarke Quotes. BrainyQuote. Retrieved September 20, 2020, from https://www.brainyquote.com/quotes/john_henrik_clarke_212006

14. *Bezos, J.* (2017, July 5). Advertising is the price you pay for having an unremarkable product or service. Linkedin.Com. https://www.linkedin.com/pulse/advertising-price-you-pay-havig-unremarkable-product-tom-fearn

15. *Bard, Alexander & Soderqvist, Jan.* (2018) Digital Libido. [E-book] Stockholm: Futurica Media,

16. Consumers Want More Creative Variety from Brand Advertising. (2020, December 2). Celtra. https://celtra.com/blog/consumers-want-more-creative-variety-from-brand-advertising/

17. *Marcuse, H.* (n.d.). Herbert Marcuse Quote. Lib Quotes. Retrieved August 15, 2020, from https://libquotes.com/herbert-marcuse/quote/lbx6b3a

18. *Lee, Michael.* Creative Director Oatly. Quote from a Social Minds podcast interview. June 2020.

19. *Chernov, J.* (n.d.). *Good Marketing vs Great Marketing.* Gracious Quotes., from https://graciousquotes.com/marketing/

Endnotes

20. *Lee, Michael.* Creative Director Oatly. Quote from a Social Minds podcast interview. June 2020.

21. *Schwab, K.* (2018, September 27). See Mailchimp's weird new branding. Fast Company. https://www.fastcompany.com/90241616/see-mailchimps-weird-new-branding

22. *Verma, S.* (2021, March 30). 40+ Walt Disney Quotes on Life, Inspiration and Dreams. QuotedText. https://quotedtext.com/walt-disney-quotes/

23. *GaryVee.* (2018, April 20). Think of Yourself as a Media Company | Meeting with Jason Khalipa. YouTube. https://www.youtube.com/watch?v=16kKNHoSwS4&t=872s

24. *Wisdom 2.0.* (2016, March 4). The Power of Social Media to Educate & Entertain | Ryan Higa | Wisdom 2.0. YouTube. https://www.youtube.com/watch?v=m1mS7Ew9jBQ&t=6s

25. *Vizard, S.* (n.d.). Measuring the magic: Why brands need to refocus on the effectiveness of creativity. Marketing week. Com. Retrieved 11 January 2021, from https://www.marketingweek.com/measuring-effectiveness-creativity-marketing/

My next book will be about creativity.
You might want to buy it. You might not.

If you do, see matsperson.com for updates.

www.ingramcontent.com/pod-product-compliance
Lightning Source LLC
Chambersburg PA
CBHW040111180526
45172CB00010B/1305